Rock Your HOLIDAYS

Three simple steps to having fun while getting things done!

ALEGRE RAMOS
NATASCHA CORRIGAN

BOOKS BY THE AUTHORS

If you aren't sure where to start, may we suggest beginning with **Rock Your Morning** followed by **3-2-1-Done.** We consider these books, and their concepts, to be foundational.

TIME MANAGEMENT
- *3-2-1-Done: Three simple strategies to get your to-do list done!* (short read, productivity)
- *Rock Your Holidays: Three simple steps to having fun while getting things done!* (short read, productivity, prioritization)

LIFE DESIGN
- *Rock Your Morning: Three simple steps to take control of your morning!* (short read, self-care, habit formation, morning ritual)

VIBRANT FAMILIES
- *Rock Your Mission: Three simple steps to creating a family mission!* (short read, family communication, value prioritization)

Alegre Ramos & Natascha Corrigan

BEYOND YOUR WILDEST DREAMS
bywd

Copyright 2023 Beyond Your Wildest Dreams (BYWD)
Published by Wild Dreamers Publishing
ISBN: 978-1-947420-30-4

All rights reserved. No part of this publication may be reproduced, stored in a retrieval system, or transmitted in any forms or by any means currently existing or yet to be developed – for example but not limited to electronic, photocopy, recording – without the prior written permission of the publisher. The only exception is quotations of three sentences or less in reviews.

Dedication

For our moms, the original Magicmakers.
~NC & AR

And to every parent struggling to balance your well-being with bringing the sparkle to your kids' lives, this is for you!

Table of Contents

Welcome! 7

What's Your Why? 12

   Exercise 1: Reason for the Season 14

Step 1: Happy All Your Days! 24

Step 2: What's Really Important 85

Step 3: Plan It Out 60

Become a Holiday Planning Whiz 67

If You Enjoyed This Book 77

Our Gifts to You 82

About The Authors 84

We'd Love to Stay in Touch! 85

You Deserve a Magical Holiday Season…Too!

Welcome!

Hello Friend,

Good for you for picking up this book today. It shows that you are ready to stop "surviving" the holidays and ready to start thriving during them!

Many people don't recognize that they have the power to change their lives. They think "the holidays are crazy and that's just how it is," completely giving up their personal power. When you do this, you are putting the "locus of control" outside of you, or externally. This way of thinking -- and the helplessness that accompanies it -- is picked up in childhood and accepted as fact as we grow up. It's a learned behavior. And just as helplessness is a learned behavior, so is its opposite: resourcefulness, also known as having an "internal locus of control".

Knowing that you have the ability to change your life opens you up to limitless possibilities.

And that's what we are all about…empowering moms, dads, and caregivers to the limitless possibilities of life by teaching you to harness the power of planning so you can prioritize yourself, save time, and accomplish your goals.

While the skills we cover in this book will work for anyone, we look at everything through the lens of being a caregiver because we know that when you have other people who make claims on your time, it can be easy to push your needs further and further down the priority list -- especially when they are cute and cuddly.

This is DOUBLY true during the holidays when many parents white-knuckle their way through to give their family the "perfect insert-holiday-here". And many of us do this while also sacrificing our own happiness, figuring that the stress and exhaustion that come with it are our lot in life. But guess what, the holidays can be fun for you too, and while we don't like to "should on" our readers, we believe this magical season *should* be fun for you. After all, if you are having fun, chances are your family will as well, because -- as many movies have demonstrated for us -- screaming your way through the holidays isn't fun for anyone.

In this book we are going to show you how to plan for the holiday season in a way that reduces stress and increases fun for everyone, but especially for you. Our goal for this book is that when the holidays are all wrapped up (pun intended), you will remember them as enjoyable and manageable, rather than something that you need to recover from.

Now we know we are all in different places in life, so as we tell our students frequently: take what speaks to you and leave the rest. Hopefully you'll return to this short-read regularly and maybe you'll pick up something from it that you didn't get the first time around. As the saying goes "when the student is ready, the master appears".

Before we go any further, we'd like to emphasize the importance of not just reading this book, but doing the exercises in it. Studies show that we don't just learn by reading, but by doing!

> ✓ **Bonus Tip:** *The best way to minimize stress is to fight it before it begins by planning things rather than just letting them happen, according to stress management and psychology research Dr. Robert Epstein.*

And now let the fun begin!

What's Your Why?

"Why do I need to do one more thing this holiday season?"

We hear you. You have a full and interesting life and reading this book and doing its exercises feels like just another thing to do. However, to paraphrase productivity expert Brian Tracy, **one minute of planning saves ten minutes of doing**. That's 1,000% percent return on your investment! Isn't it worth it to spend an hour on this book and save ten hours later? Truthfully, you'll likely save much more time because this book will really "level up" your planning game.

We like to say, planning makes everything better. And our students agree:

- "I did the *Turn Your To-do List into Your To-Done List* [workshop] and in one hour learned some simple and practical ways to help eliminate the overwhelm that I feel when I look at what I need/want to do for the week." ~Allie
- "I feel much more in control of, and committed to, the process." ~Sarah
- "I have learned so much that I have been implementing daily to help keep me on track." ~Michelle

Not only will it save you time, an hour spent "pre-gaming" your holiday season will save you a ton of stress later when unpredictable things arise in an already stretched schedule. Hopefully you see why this book is going to be your best friend for the next hour, so let's jump in.

Exercise 1: Reason for the Season

Close your eyes, take a deep breath …deeper, exhale and get in touch with the feeling of how you want your holiday season to *feel*. What's a word or phrase that captures your "reason for the season"?

Maybe it comes from a feeling place. Who do you see yourself being? How do you want to show up for you? For your family? Some examples of this could be:

- I am peaceful and it radiates out to my family too.
- I am enveloped in connection.
- Fun is how we do it!

Or maybe you prefer to think in terms of activities rather than feelings. Maybe your ideal season is full of parties, or puzzles, or long sits by the fireplace? Here are some examples to get you thinking:

- I want to maximize memory-making opportunities with my family sprinkled with a couple of large events with lots of people.
- I want to spend time with my closest friends attending every social-media worthy event within five miles.
- I want my holidays to be relaxing.
- My ideal holiday season is spent in worship and reflection.
- I'd like a week of spontaneous doing followed by a week of locking myself up with books.
- My "reason for the season" is cooking and staying home.
- I want to have fun and stay on budget.

There's no right answer, just the right one for you and your family.

Write your thoughts down in the space provided on the next page.

Rock Your Holidays: Three simple steps to having fun while getting things done!

Whatever you wrote is your "Why", your "reason for the season" and it will act as your internal compass as you create your holiday plan, guiding you in making choices, and get you back on track when things get overwhelming. When you're loaded up with invitations, stymied by options, and being pulled in different directions, your *Why* will help you maintain boundaries and provide you with the clarity to be true to yourself.

Hopefully you wrote down something really compelling because the more excited you are about your *Why*, the more likely you are to stick with your plan.

Committing to your *Why* will keep you focused as the dizzying array of holiday offerings tempt you to overcommit, overspend, and overextend yourself.

Why would you say yes to five parties if you just want to stay home and cook? You

might be thinking, "But I *should* go to the parties." To which we would reply, "Stop shoulding on yourself!" Life is too short to do things because you think you should. Granted, there is some give and take when you are part of a larger family unit, however, we'll get to some ideas for how to avoid doing things you don't want to do because shoulding eventually catches up with you and turns into resentment. Keeping your *Why* in mind will help you stop the shoulding before it begins.

For example, if you want your holidays to be relaxing, and you don't find parties or large events relaxing, then you can easily say "no" when you receive invitations to these. If you

have a defined holiday budget and a friend invites you for a ski weekend that is beyond that, again, you can easily decline because you've already committed to your finances.

The first step of getting what you want is knowing what you want.

Your *Why* will also make it easy to recognize the opportunities you don't want to miss out on because you've defined your goals clearly. Having clarity about what you want makes setting and maintaining boundaries so much easier.

We recommend writing your *Why* on a small piece of paper or index card and taping it on your bathroom mirror, or a kitchen cabinet, or using it as a bookmark. Put it somewhere you will see it often to help keep you on track. Also, find a place to keep this book handy throughout the holidays to remind you of what it is you said you wanted to do.

Holidaze

♪ It's the most wonderful time of the year ♪ …but is it really?

According to a Healthline survey, 62% of American adults report that their stress levels are "very or somewhat" elevated during the holiday season. American women feel this stress more than men which is probably because they also report shouldering more of the responsibility for holiday shopping and planning. Whether it's trying to find the perfect gift for everyone -- even those little "hostess gifts" add up -- and make sure they are ordered in time or getting cards out with the adorable, annual family photo that you booked, styled, and shot with a photographer a month earlier. Making everything "just so" is a lot of work -- fun work, yes, but work nonetheless.

It's beginning to look a lot like…busy.

As we write this book, we'd like to acknowledge a couple things upfront. The first is that just by reading this book, you are in a blessed position, having the time and means available to consider how to make your holiday season less stressed and more joyous. Writing this book reminds us that we have much to be grateful for, and perhaps you'd like to take a moment to feel grateful as well.

Secondly, the goal of this book -- and of all our books really -- is not to help you stuff more things onto the calendar. No

matter how well-planned a solidly booked calendar is, if it feels stressful, you're doing too much. Instead, we want to give you a framework to think about "What's really important to me" and to ensure that you are spending your time doing what you want to do and not what you think you "should" do.

So, grab a cup o' cocoa, or tea, or vino and let's pre-game this sucker!

Step 1: Happy All Your Days!

(aka Brain Dump)

We luuuuuurv the holidays: the seasonal events, the special meals, the extra time with family. Our mothers did an amazing job making them magical for us and we happily endeavor to do the same for our families. Of course, it's not without its challenges.

A big part of what makes this time of year so hectic are all the special events that pop up: light shows, seasonal performances, neighborhoods that "go all out". Couple those with family, school and work events, and it all starts to add up…quickly. Throw in some cookie making and a gift bazaar or three and suddenly it's hard to figure out how you are going to get "normal life" done too. Wouldn't it be great if we could just clone ourselves and do all the things?

But we can't.

However, there's no need to decide what you are and aren't going to do this second. Right now, you're just going to think about what **want** to do. Don't worry about what's realistic, we're just going to go for it as though everything is possible.

Step one in our "tame your holidays" process is to list every possible thing you want to do between October and January-ish: cookies, drive to the snow, eggnog, caroling, light shows, theme parks, concerts, snow shoeing, making garland, sledding, whatever…write it all down. Feel free to add

Nowruz and Lunar New Year or anything else. Don't worry about how you're going to make it work, just think "pie in the sky".

✏️ **Set a timer for ten minutes and write down** everything you want to do during the holidays. Do not censor yourself, now is the time for brain dumping, no editing allowed.

Don't skip this step! Studies show that writing things down releases the brain chemical dopamine which makes you feel satisfied. It also clears your brain--think of it like closing open windows on your computer--which reduces anxiety and frees up brain space to do higher level thinking which is where we'll be headed with steps two and three.

Rock Your Holidays: Three simple steps to having fun while getting things done!

Here are our own holiday activity wish lists in case you want some ideas of where to begin.

ALEGRE'S HOLIDAY WISH LIST

October
- Homeschool trunk or treat
- Buy Nothing trunk or treat
- Make family costumes
- Trick or Treat
- Hand out candy
- Decorate house, set-up ofrenda
- Decorate muertos skulls
- Go to a pumpkin patch
- Go to a party or two
- Holiday card photo shoot
- Camping trip or one-week vacation

November
- Bizcation with Natascha
- Teach a Harness the Power of Planning course
- Order holiday cards and annual Christmas tree ornament
- Decorate house for Thanksgiving
- Leftovers Potluck Friendsgiving
- Host Thanksgiving dinner
- Make food for Thanksgiving
- Thanksgiving Day sunrise costume onesie hike
- Put Christmas tree up
- Decorate house for Christmas
- Thanksgiving with family
- Day after Thanksgiving popovers
- Victorian Ball

December
- Kiddo's Christmas concert
- Attend Nutcracker ballet
- Attend a holiday light show
- Make tamales
- Bake cookies
- Mail out cookies
- Send out holiday cards
- Make eggnog
- Visit decorated houses near grandma
- Christmas Tea with friends
- Church Christmas program
- Adopt a child via church
- Decorate Rose Parade float
- Go to Disneyland
- Alegre's Chorale Group concert and tea
- Holiday Bazaar
- Go to a party or two
- Read "A Christmas Carol"
- ~~Work party~~

January-ish

- Watch Rose Parade
- Make New Year danish
- Make dumplings
- Plan Chinese New Year brunch
- Set up tangerines and li-see for Chinese New Year
- Attend a Lunar New Year event
- Ski trip

Rock Your Holidays: Three simple steps to having fun while getting things done!

NATASCHA'S HOLIDAY WISH LIST

October
- Go to Knott's Scary Farm
- Finish making (or purchase) kids' costumes
- Attend Halloween carnival at school
- Trick or Treat with the Lopez family
- Go to the Katz's Scary Stories 'Round the Campfire party
- Visit the haunted houses on the Haunted House Competition list
- Photo shoot for holiday cards (scheduled in September)
- Decorate house
- Carve pumpkins
- Birthday party for eldest kiddo
- Anniversary dinner (yes, we have 2 birthdays and an anniversary in Oct)
- Pumpkin picking at local farm

November
- Turkey Trot fundraiser for shelter
- Birthday party or dinner for hubby
- Tree trimming open house party
- Order holiday cards
- Take the kids shopping to spend their "give" money for the food bank
- Watch Thanksgiving Day Parade
- Attend LA Auto Show
- Make side dishes for Friendsgiving
- Decorate inside/outside house for Tree trimming party
- Complete ordering gifts for family
- Attend an Operation Christmas Shoebox packing event
- Attend Holiday in the Park

December
- Attend LA Comic-Con
- Finalize all gifts sent to Christmas destination
- Send out Holiday cards

December (con't)

- Attend annual White Elephant party
- Attend annual fancy adult-only holiday party
- Attend Gingerbread House Decorating party
- Adopt a Giving Tree kid at church
- Travel to Omi and Grandpa's
- Skiing
- Snow-shoeing
- Visit Church Street
- Visit Museum Light Show
- Attend Polar Express Show
- Watch 4 holiday movies

January-ish

- Ice skating Downtown

Step 2: What's Really Important

(aka Prioritize)

Now that you've listed everything you want to do, we want you to spend some time prioritizing them. Taking the time to rate holiday activities might seem like a needless use of time, however, as many productivity experts can attest, spending a little bit of time planning saves you lots of time in doing.

If you don't identify your priorities, you'll treat everything with the same importance. This is what lands you in overwhelm, saying "yes" to every ask that comes your way. As you prioritize, keep your ***Why*** in mind because this is how you'll get the holiday season you desire, by keeping your holiday compass pointed at your goal.

For example, here's Alegre's December list rated on a 1 to 3 importance scale with 1 being something she definitely wants to do.

Alegre: *My "reason for the season" is to make memories and keep holiday traditions alive while also engaging in a handful of "outside of the house" events. We enjoy a couple of lowkey parties, but that's enough for us. Our family loves Disneyland during the holidays, but it isn't something we want to do every year which is why I ranked it a "3". Also, the Christmas Eve program at our church is special, but it's the same from year to year so depending on what date our* *extended family can get together -- Christmas Eve versus Christmas Day -- we might skip it. Feel free to follow my lead and write how often you want to do an activity if it's something you want to do regularly but not every year.*

December
- Kiddo's Christmas concert 1
- Attend Nutcracker ballet 2
- December light shows 2, at least every other year
- Make tamales 1
- Bake cookies 1
- Mail out cookies 2, only to two family members who aren't local
- Send out holiday cards 2
- Make eggnog 2
- Visit decorated houses near grandma 2
- Christmas Tea with friends 1
- Christmas Eve program at church 3, once in a while
- Adopt a child via church 2
- Decorate Rose Parade float 3, every 2-3 years
- Go to Disneyland 3, at least every 2-3 years
- Alegre's Chorale Group concert and tea 1
- Holiday Bazaar 2

- Go to a party or two 3
- Read "A Christmas Carol" 1
- Work party 0 (I'll explain why I gave this a 0 below)

✏️ **Your turn! Rate your holiday activity list using a 1 through 3 system.** Re-read your *Why* to reinforce what it is you want for this season. As you go through this exercise you might also decide that there are holiday activities that you like to do regularly but don't have to happen every year. Feel free to note that next to the item. Our rating system guideline is:

> 1 = "I would never miss this"
> 2 = "I'd love to make this happen"
> 3 = "Fun but if we skip it, it's no big deal"

After you rate your activities, you might realize that you don't even want to give something a 3. Perhaps you feel it is not worth your time, energy, or money because it's not aligned with your *Why*. Personal insight for the win! Feel free to cross those things out or perhaps notate a time in the future when you might do that activity again.

***Alegre:** When my kiddo was very young, we did fewer things during the holidays because I didn't have the mental or physical energy. Give yourself the grace to recognize when you do and don't have the bandwidth for things.*

Also, rating the importance of your activities makes it easy to make hard choices later on. For instance, if going to your kid's holiday show is a 1 and you are invited to attend an unexpected work party that same day, it reminds you of the importance of the commitment you've made to your kiddo. Choosing your priorities based on your priorities and values is a better way to ensure big picture satisfaction than choosing to do something because it "sounds fun" in the moment or you *could* fit it in or you feel that you "should" do the thing. It helps create clear boundaries that are easier for you to follow because of how defined they are. It's so easy to say "no" to things when you take the time to figure out what you value.

***Alegre:** I rate "work party" as a zero because it's something that we decided long ago was not a priority. While we did attend one when my husband was new to the company, it just wasn't our thing and the organization doesn't make attendance mandatory. For years we would fret over whether we should attend, however, we kept skipping it until one year we agreed that we would stop even considering it. Taking it off our holiday list meant we could stop having the* *"should we or shouldn't we" discussion every year and freed up mental energy for other things. Don't underestimate how liberating and peace-giving it can be to take things off your list. Thoughts are energy. If you don't have to think about something you are saving yourself energy you can use elsewhere.*

Another benefit of rating the activities is that items that you gave a 3 can act as "pressure valves" that you do during years when you have more time, energy, or money, and don't do those years when you need more space. You don't have to do every activity every year for it to be a meaningful tradition and prioritizing them helps to clarify which ones you can skip from time to time and still have an enjoyable season.

> The key is not to prioritize your schedule, but to schedule your priorities.
> ~Stephen Covey

Alegre: *I tend to be a very educationally-focused kind of parent which is reinforced by the fact that I homeschool my child. I'm always trying to find the "teachable moment" in every situation. When my child was eight or nine, she said something to me that didn't feel good. I don't remember the exact words but it was something like, "You're the parent who teaches me and Dad is the parent I have fun with."*

After thinking about it for a bit, that conversation initiated two changes in our house. The first was that I asked my partner to be more active in the teaching/disciplining side of life. I'm no longer the only one making sure our child is doing her part to contribute to the household.

Secondly, I made a point to schedule regular Mommy-Daughter days (MMDs) where the focus would be on just being together. Sometimes we'll go to a trampoline park or a flea market or the beach, but the point is fun and that's a helpful mind-shift for me because I get so used to focusing on her education.

I've often found in life that a person's greatest strength can also be their greatest weakness. I saw this in my own father who was great at sharing information in a one-sided way, but struggled to have conversations because in his work he did a lot of lecturing. At family dinners, he'd complain that our family interrupted him and didn't understand that it wasn't normal to speak for twenty minutes straight.

We schedule a year's worth of MMDs in December for the coming year. This is part of Beyond Your Wildest Dreams' -- the name of our business -- process for setting up an annual planner. We teach our students to make space for the things that are important to you before your calendar fills up with requests from others. Date nights and MMDs don't happen without planning. However, by the time June rolls around, other opportunities have cropped up that sometimes come into competition with my MMDs.

However, because I'm very clear about my values -- I have eight values ranked in hierarchical order that sit in the pocket of my planner at all times -- it's easy for me to say "no" to anything that interferes with my kiddo. Having my values predetermined and in hierarchical order helps me set clear, defined boundaries and show up as the person I want to be.

There have been moments when I've considered skipping a MMD because my daughter hasn't remembered -- she doesn't look at her planner regularly enough yet to always notice -- and I'm tired or could use the time for work. Those are the moments when I realize how razor-thin the line is between living my values and doing what's easy. I value these moments for reminding me of what's important and the fact that showing up as the person I want to be is a choice

I have to recommit to regularly. That being said, I have occasionally rescheduled our MDD with my kiddo's blessing, however, they always happen.

Natascha: *I have a tough time making decisions. I used to chalk it up to being a Libra. Crack open any horoscope book and it tells us Libras that we'd make great judges or mediators, because we can easily see both, or sometimes all, sides of an issue and that we are very fair-minded. While that might be great career advice (which I did not take), it makes for a very conflicted existence. I would often say "yes" to anything and everything because even if I maybe only kinda wanted to do it, I could see how it could be fun.*

Let me tell you, I balked at the idea of ranking activities. I break out in hives just thinking about having to make decisions about what things are more important than others. Especially when it comes to my kiddos and them having the most magical holiday season possible.

But taking the time to think about and rate each of our holiday activities through the lens of my Why has made all the difference in sussing out what's important, what to say "yes" to and what to say "no" to. It's reduced the stress of having to make decisions about what to fit into the calendar. Plus, it gives me guidance when I'm about to be flummoxed by a last-minute invitation to join a carolers performance that weekend.

Once you have each month's activities ranked, the next thing to do is consider the steps required to make that thing happen. Not everything will have multiple steps, but many do.

For the sake of example, we're going to pick one of the more challenging activities to illustrate all the steps that can be required to make a holiday event happen: a trip to a theme park. Theme parks have become popular destinations with the advent of holiday-themed decor, shows, and activities. However, unlike other activities, making plans to visit a theme park, even if it's local, can be like planning for a mini-vacation both in cost and complexity. This is because it includes a lot of "invisible work" that can go unnoticed by your family.

Holiday activity: Go to Disneyland in December for two days and stay three nights at a local hotel to maximize the time in the park.

1. **January-December:** Decide on a budget and regularly put money aside. (***Alegre:*** *In December our family discusses how often we'd like to go camping, travel, and whether or not we'll be going to Disneyland the following year since all of these things take time away from the other. We then pencil in dates for when these will happen and budget accordingly.)*

2. **July 1:** Pick December dates as early as possible but by July at the latest. This often includes a lot of reminding on the part of Alegre because her husband doesn't feel the same urgency to plan in advance. As he pushes off picking a date, she reminds him that

they've agreed she's the planner in the family, but that all the fun things he likes to do require forethought. Eventually, a date gets picked (hallelujah!), however, not without Alegre expending a fair amount of energy, although, it does seem to be getting better, year by year (progress!).

3. **July 2:** Hubby asks for time off work. Alegre makes sure to reschedule any standing commitments she may have.

4. **July 7:** Once time off is approved, make hotel reservations.

5. **August:** Purchase tickets and reserve the dates in December *(these open up four months before your desired date).*

6. **November:** Make any special reservations for restaurants or special shows at Disneyland *(these open up 60 days before your ticket reservation date).*

7. **December:** Go to Disneyland.

Let's compare that with a more "typical" holiday activity such as hosting Thanksgiving dinner. Whether you are planning a dinner for four or fourteen, a multi-course, high-expectation meal like Thanksgiving requires some foresight.

Holiday activity: Host Thanksgiving Dinner

1. **Early October:** Decide to host Thanksgiving dinner for people who live locally *(if you are inviting people to visit, the timeframe will be longer).* For Alegre this requires back and forth with her mother because they take turns hosting holiday events. Alegre may have to

convince hubby if she really wants to host and he's not feeling it, reminding him that part of the joy of the holidays for her is cooking and hosting loved ones.

2. **Mid-October:** Consider if we'll be inviting people outside immediate family.

3. **One month before Thanksgiving:** Invite guests

4. **First two weeks of November:** Put together menu, decorate house (enlist help from family)

5. **Five days before Thanksgiving:** First grocery trip, start setting table (enlist help from family)

6. **Three days before Thanksgiving:** Second grocery trip (there's always more than one)

7. **Two days before Thanksgiving:** Final "just in case I forgot something" grocery trip. Sometimes Alegre will do this as a grocery delivery to save time.

8. **Day before Thanksgiving:** Cook or par-cook as much as possible (enlist help from family), finish setting table (enlist help from family)

9. **Thanksgiving:** Finish cooking (enlist help from family), leave an hour to compose oneself/shower/dress

10. **Day after Thanksgiving:** Clean up (enlist help from family) and make fresh popovers for breakfast (a favorite tradition).

Your turn! List the steps required for any activity that has multiple components. As you are listing the steps, make notes if there are things people can help you with. Everyone who derives joy from the event is someone who can help contribute to making it happen. Don't feel like you have to do everything alone. Humans are not mind-readers, so don't expect others to help if you don't ask.

Alegre*: My father never lifted a finger to help around the house. The gender-based division of labor was especially noticeable at Thanksgiving dinner when the men of my family would retire to watch football while the women did clean-up. In my experience, unspoken divisions of labor like that frequently lead to resentment. If you want a more honest, kind, sustainable partnership, teach your family that loving a person means being helpful, and that if they eat the food, they are welcome and able to help cook and clean too.*

We recommend planning out the steps in order of your prioritization, so tackle the 1s first, then 2s, then 3s. We like doing it this way because you might get to the 3s and think "Oh my gosh, I'm already exhausted, forget the rest of these activities" to which we say "HUZZAH!" Deciding what NOT to do is a wonderfully liberating thing.

Alegre Ramos & Natascha Corrigan

Rock Your Holidays: Three simple steps to having fun while getting things done!

Alegre Ramos & Natascha Corrigan

Rock Your Holidays: Three simple steps to having fun while getting things done!

You don't get what you want.
You get what you prioritize.

Step 3: Plan It Out

(aka: Calendar)

Congratulations, you've made it to step three which is where things get really fun. The first step had you taking holiday planning out of your head and put it on paper. Step two was to prioritize and think through a plan for some of the bigger activities with multiple steps. Step three is where you take your plans and put them in time by calendaring them.

Before we have you do this, we do have a few tips to help this process.

- **Avoid "shoulding" on yourself.** We know we wrote about this earlier, but it bears repeating. Caregivers get "shoulded on" a lot by society and our families, however, in our experience trying to live up to everyone's expectations just leads to burn-out and resentment. Keeping your *Why* in mind is one of the best ways to not give in to the shoulding. Erect a mental boundary around yourself powered by your desires for what you want your holidays to be like and then maintain it by reminding yourself of what IS and ISN'T a priority.

Related to this, if you have a regular self-care routine, we recommend keeping up with it as much as possible. Avoid sacrificing your self-care in the pursuit of adding more to your calendar. You will show up as your best self this holiday season when you have met your mental/physical/spiritual needs. As we like to say, "self-care is healthcare". For more on creating a habit of self-care, get our short workbook ***Rock Your Morning,*** which is all about creating a morning ritual. For a great article on how important self-care is, we recommend this one from Prevention Magazine at tinyURL.com/PreventionSC

- **Divide and conquer.** Kids have a lot of energy. They want to do *all* the things, but that doesn't mean you have to as well! This is where friends and family can help out. Maybe you love the light shows but don't love to bake, but your kiddo wants to. Maybe you have a friend or family member who loves baking. If they have kids, ask for a swap: you do the lightshow they do baking. If they don't have kiddos, see if they would enjoy hosting yours for cookies. It's great for a kid to have a chance to develop relationships with all the adults in her life and it gives the adults a chance to rest (yay sleep!).

Alegre: *My hubby and I do this all the time. He and my daughter love doing car stuff together (not my cup of tea) and my daughter and I do things that we both enjoy. My mom pitches in too sometimes taking our daughter to things that I don't mind missing. We also have a couple of families that we are close to that we'll divide and conquer with.*

- **Keep fun, fun!** The whole point of our book is to ensure that YOU have fun. Eff invisible work. Eff being taken for granted. Eff sacrificing yourself on the altar of your family so that they can have a magical holiday season at your expense. **You. Deserve. To Enjoy. Yourself. As Well.** So, when all else fails, when you wonder if you "should" (there's that word we hate) do something, ask yourself, "Is this fun for me?" The holidays should be fun for you too, so keep fun, fun! If it's not fun, don't do it. Your lower blood pressure will thank you -- and us -- for this.

Alegre: This single principle has brought so much more joy, peace, and time into my life. I first came up with it when I was planning my wedding and things were on the train to "Notfunville". I reminded myself that I deserved to enjoy my special day as much as my guests and because of this, I prioritized the parts of my wedding, focused on what mattered, and ended up having a fan-tastic time. Also, keep in mind that things change. When my daughter was little, I didn't bake cookies during the holidays because it felt overwhelming. As she's become more independent, I've added back things that I had put on hold. What's not fun now, might become fun later, so if you enjoy something -- but don't have the bandwidth for it -- keep it on your list of things you'd like to do, but remember that doesn't mean you have to do it every year.

Natascha: *One December my cousin gifted our family an Elf on the Shelf book and companion elf doll. I knew that many of my friends enjoyed the tradition of making up mischievous scenarios for their own personal Buddy to get into each night and their kids to find each morning. Hey, it sounds like it would be a hoot! I just knew it was something that would have felt like a "have-to" after a while and that it would fall squarely on my shoulders. That particular brand of holiday magic was not in alignment with my reason for the season. I thanked my cousin and promptly donated it. It was several years before the boys asked why we didn't have an elf who* *lived in our house that reported to Santa. I said,*

"Yeah...we just don't, Sweetie."

✏️ **Crack open the last three months of your planner** or use the calendars provided on the following pages, and start penciling things in. You've already done the hard part - getting in touch with your *Why* and the deep thinking associated with prioritizing. You've also teased out any activities that have multiple steps. Now it's time to put those activities in time by calendaring them. Walk any of the steps needed for the activities backward and put them in too. This will drastically reduce feeling like an event crept up on you. But when we say pencil, we mean pencil. This gives you the flexibility to change your mind, move things around, and keep your calendar neat enough to be legible.

And if at any point in the calendaring you start feeling overwhelmed, look at your "reason for the season" and see if this activity is contributing to it. If not, consider not doing that thing. Keep fun, fun!

A little more sparkle,
a little less stress
This holiday season,
we wish you the best.

OCTOBER

SUN	MON	TUE	WED	THU	FRI	SAT

Rock Your Holidays: Three simple steps to having fun while getting things done!

NOVEMBER

SUN	MON	TUE	WED	THU	FRI	SAT

DECEMBER

SUN	MON	TUE	WED	THU	FRI	SAT

Rock Your Holidays: Three simple steps to having fun while getting things done!

JANUARY-ISH

SUN	MON	TUE	WED	THU	FRI	SAT

Become a Holiday Planning Whiz

We have some more helpful suggestions beyond the three steps outlined in this book we'd like to share that can create even more peace and space in your holiday season.

1. **Rinse and repeat.** Keep the calendar you created for next year and the year after. Use it as a jumping off point. Your *Why* may shift, things will change, your family will go through different stages and you can update your holiday plan as needed, but either way, it's a great starting point.
2. **Make invisible work, visible!** It can be frustrating when all your hard work goes unnoticed, however, people aren't mind-readers. Let's take a page from the office space where you have to give your manager updates on what you're working on. If you are feeling taken for granted, talk about it. Perhaps you can start with, "I'd like our family to have a wonderful holiday season. I'm hoping we can bake cookies, go to the snow, and visit the grandparents; however, I can't do it alone. How can you help make these things happen so I don't feel overwhelmed and like I have to do all the work and can't enjoy the holidays too?"

3. **Don't reinvent the wheel**. Is there an event or task that you do each year that basically has the same set of steps, ingredients, guests, etc.? When you take on that task or throw that event this year, be sure to create the shopping list, guest list, to-do-lists and save it in a document or note on your mobile device. It saves a ton of time and energy and your future self will thank you.

Natascha: Our family throws a tree-trimming party the Sunday after Thanksgiving every year. It motivates us to get our home yuletide ready and gives us an excuse to see our friends before December pulls all our spheres in different directions. After the second time we did this, I realized I was making more work for myself recreating the lists for everything that needed to be done, bought and prepared. I made a master list specifically for the party. It includes all the food and beverages, plus any recipes needed, a shopping list (organized by store) and house to-dos to get it party-ready. I update it regularly. If we ran out of a certain item early in the party or there was a bunch of one thing leftover, I made a note and adjust the quantity for next year. In recent years, I've divided the pre-party to-dos by family member now that my kiddos are older and can take on more responsibility. It makes the party prepping much easier and pleasant for me and the whole family.

4. **Feel free to edit as you go.** Imagine this - you're halfway through November with apple picking behind you and Thanksgiving week looming. You did an excellent job pre-gaming prior to the holiday season kicking in. You established your ***Why***, did the braindump and figured out your last three months of the year. Maybe you even calendered most of your 3s, along with those must-have 1s and would-be-nice 2s. Everything you put in seemed totally doable…then. But now you're looking at your calendar and you're feeling overwhelmed. It happens.

   Humans tend to feel very optimistic about our future self, which is a good thing. But researchers have found that we can also overextend our poor future self -- also referred to as our should self (there's that word again) -- and assign ourselves more to do than we can realistically handle.

Of course, it'd be great if your past self hadn't put you in this position in the first place, but if you find yourself stretched thin, we give you permission to decline an invitation even after you RSVPed "yes". Go ahead get some store-bought cookies for the holiday potluck instead of making them from scratch. It's fine. And maybe jot down a note next to that activity so you'll remember this lesson learned for next year.

Even the best plans will require a "course correct" from time to time, especially something as fluid as the holiday season where new opportunities continue to pop-up as it progresses. Being mentally prepared to course correct is a valuable mental tool in and of itself because some of us have a hard time letting go of a plan once it's created.

Also, Stoic philosophy – Alegre's a fan! – has a principle called negative visualization which basically means preparing for the worst. Some people – Alegre among them – find it calming to prepare for the worst. In this case, the "worst" that you are preparing for is that you might have to adjust your plan. However, knowing in advance that you might have to do this means you won't be surprised when you've been swimming along and suddenly you feel like your plan isn't working for you. If or when that happens, just take a deep breath and reconnect with your *Why* – your compass – and adjust accordingly.

We've given you all our best advice to make this a season to remember, so go forth and Rock Your Holidays! We'd love to hear how it goes. Send us a message at hello@bywdreams.com.

This holiday season, keep your loved ones close and receipts for all major purchases closer.

If You Enjoyed This Book

Then you'd probably love *Harness the Power of Planning,* our flagship "life by design, not default" online course. It is available as a live, two-day event once a year or as on-demand videos. **Find out more at** BYWDreams.com

Harness the Power of Planning is built on two premises. The first is a maxim credited to a couple different productivity experts: **For every one minute of planning, you'll save ten minutes of doing**. That's a 1000% return on investment and it's the reason why we believe planning is so valuable, because who doesn't want more time?

Secondly, our goal is not to turn anyone into a productivity robot. We want our students to live richer lives, to have more of whatever it is that they want whether it's more naps, more cuddles, more sunrise hikes…whatever. If what you want is more being, and less doing, we are all for it. Afterall, we are human beings, not human doings.

Which leads us to the second premise and bonus tip.

> ✓ ***Bonus tip:*** *You can have everything you want in life with **70% effort**. That would be a C- in school, but in life, it's an absolute A+ because big goals are achieved with consistency over a long time. 100% effort isn't sustainable over a long time, but 70% is.*

We know this 70% effort works because we built our business, Beyond Your Wildest Dreams, with just a little bit of time here and there, in between play dates and swim parties with our kids.

Did we make every deadline we set? NO!

Did we make mistakes and pivot? YES!

But we did 70% of what we said we would, over a long period of time, and that's the secret.

If you are:

- Trying to figure out how to be more organized? We can help.
- Trying to figure out how to get in more self-care? We can help.
- Trying to figure out what to do with the rest of your life? We can help.

Here are some testimonials from our alumni.

I wish I had taken this training in my 20s! This is such a powerful seminar on planning. I could methodically align my values with my goals for the next 20 years. **_I thought I was good at planning, however, this course took me to the next level._** *~Luz S.*

The natural skeptic in me wasn't sure what to expect from BYWD. It exceeded my expectations. When you follow the process and do the homework, **_it's nothing short of lifechanging._** *I've been empowered with invaluable tools and will absolutely take it again! ~Julie L.*

BYWD has been one of the greatest gifts I've given myself. *The beauty of it is that even when life throws you curve balls, it is so easy to course correct and get back on track.* **_Alegre & Natascha have taken a concept that has eluded me my whole life and broken it down into really simple, doable steps_** *that just make sense. I would definitely recommend the course to anyone who wants to be more intentional with their life and their dreams. ~Michelle L.*

These sessions were easy to follow, provided chunks of information in bite-sized pieces, and each session built upon previous lessons. **Alegre and Natascha are engaging and fun instructors** *and are willing to help every step of the way.* **It really helped me turn my vision for the future into actionable steps I can take right now***, and for that I am so very grateful! Thank you, BYWD! ~Sarah M.*

Clarity is the best word to describe what I gained through taking the Beyond Your Wildest Dreams seminar. *Learning how to better identify and classify my goals, how to adopt measurable steps to reach those goals, and how to keep my goals and my values aligned has helped me rethink how I plan for the future. But the most concrete benefit I've experienced is shifting from 'calendaring' to 'planning.' ~Sarah B.*

I wish I had taken this course 10 years or more ago! I've made lists of goals, but I didn't really have a process for executing the actions needed to achieve the goals. **This course gives you the tools to execute your plans.** *They teach you how to plan for your life. If you follow the advice in this program, you will achieve your goals. ~Mia M.*

Our Gifts to You

Thank you for buying this book! It means the world to us to have you read it.

Please let us know you enjoyed it or learned something by **leaving us a review wherever you purchased this book.**

The stars are more important than the words, but we love the words too! And tell a friend about it, or better yet, buy the book as a gift for someone.

If you are interested in bulk purchases for your company or school, email hello@bywdreams.com. We also enjoy leading workshops, in-person or virtual, for companies and organizations. Please reach out if you'd like more information.

As a thank you for reading, we have three gifts for you:

- **Printable time-blocking worksheet**: to help you engage the keystone habit of planning your day

- **Personality Quizzes** that will help you plan better by giving you insight into yourself

- **$900 discount (originally $1299, save 70% and pay $399)** for our two-day virtual live course *Harness the Power of Planning* (sign-up for our waitlist or take the recorded version for only $47.)

To receive these gifts, please go to TinyURL.com/BYWDgifts

About The Authors

Alegre Ramos is an eco-homeschooling mamapreneur who loves camping, Korean spas, and stand-up comedy. An award-winning speaker, she'd love to fire up your audience with her message about the importance of women putting themselves first.

Natascha Corrigan lives in L.A. with her husband, their two boys, and a Danebull named Hermann.

Learn more about them and *Harness the Power of Planning* by watching this video: youtu.be/ua7o8JR64Cg

We'd Love to Stay in Touch!

- BYWDreams.com – Sign-up for our newsletter and receive our FREE Mini-course "Create Your Morning Ritual" as well as our Monthly and Annual Review templates

- Youtube.com/@BYWDreams

- Facebook.com/BYWDreams

- Instagram.com/BYWDreams

- TikTok.com/@BYWDreams

- Pinterest.com/BYWDreams

> A year from now, you'll wish you started today.
> ~Karen Lamb